ABOVE AND BEYOND

WITH

COLLABORATION

NATALIE HYDE

Crabtree Publishing Company
www.crabtreebooks.com

Author: Natalie Hyde

Series research and development: Reagan Miller

Editors: Sonya Newland, Kathy Middleton, and Janine Deschenes

Proofreader: Wendy Scavuzzo

Designer: Rocket Design Ltd

Photo researcher: Sonya Newland

Cover design: Katherine Berti

Production coordinator and prepress technician: Tammy McGarr

Print coordinator: Katherine Berti

Produced for Crabtree Publishing by White-Thomson Publishing

Photographs:
Alamy: Ben Molyneux: p. 23, WENN Ltd: p. 28b, Arterra Picture Library: p. 40b, The Art Archive: p. 43; Stefan Chabluk: p. 123, p. 41; Getty Images: Gary M. Prior: p. 36; Rocket Design: p. 32b, p. 38; Shutterstock: Mandy Godbehear: p. 4, Janos Timea: p. 5t, Macrovector: p. 5b, Camilo Torres: p. 6t, GongTo: p. 6b, docstockmedia: p. 7, Thinglass: p. 8, Pepsco Studio: p. 9, denk creative: p. 9, Nitichai: p. 10, Sindre T: p. 11t, Marina9: 11b, Arthimedes: p. 12, Yuriy Seleznev: p. 14, tuulijumala: p. 15, Aaron Amat: p. 16, elenabsl: p. 17, vetkit: pp. 18 and 19, Carolyn Franks: pp. 18–19, singkam: pp. 18 and 19, Kaponia Aliaksei: p. 18m, Mega Pixel: p. 18b, Wissanu: p. 20, Thomas Amby: p. 21t, america365: p. 21b, america365: p. 22t, Rawpixel.com: p. 22b, Pierre-Yves Babelon: p. 24, Rashad Ashurov: p. 25t, Rawpixel.com: p. 25b, pp. 44–45, Zadorozhnyi Viktor: p. 26l, Vasilius: p. 26r, DRogatnev: p. 27, Billion Photos: p. 28t, Martin Allinger: p. 29, Jezper: p. 30t, Sascha Burkard: p. 30b, Crystal Home: p. 31, VLADGRIN: p. 32t, g-stockstudio: p. 33, Soul wind: p. 34m, noche: p. 34l&r, Hiranyaa: p. 35, Magicvector: p. 37t, ChameleonsEye: p. 37b, Appolinaria: p. 39t, Protasov AN: p. 39b, Stocklifemax: p. 40t, kowition: p. 42.

All other images by Shutterstock

Library and Archives Canada Cataloguing in Publication

Hyde, Natalie, 1963-, author
    Above and beyond with collaboration / Natalie Hyde.

(Fueling your future! going above and beyond in the 21st century)
Includes index.
Issued in print and electronic formats.
ISBN 978-0-7787-2829-0 (hardback).--
ISBN 978-0-7787-2843-6 (paperback).--
ISBN 978-1-4271-1833-2 (html)

    1. Social groups--Juvenile literature. 2. Interpersonal relations--Juvenile literature. 3. Social interaction--Juvenile literature. 4. Cooperativeness--Juvenile literature. 5. Teams in workplace--Juvenile literature. I. Title.

HM716.H93 2016   j302.3   C2016-903299-X
                                         C2016-903300-7

Library of Congress Cataloging-in-Publication Data

CIP available at the Library of Congress

Crabtree Publishing Company
www.crabtreebooks.com   1-800-387-7650

Printed in Canada/082016/TL20160715

Published in Canada
Crabtree Publishing
616 Welland Ave.
St. Catharines, Ontario
L2M 5V6

Published in the United States
Crabtree Publishing
PMB 59051
350 Fifth Avenue, 59th Floor
New York, New York 10118

Published in the United Kingdom
Crabtree Publishing
Maritime House
Basin Road North, Hove
BN41 1WR

Published in Australia
Crabtree Publishing
3 Charles Street
Coburg North
VIC, 3058

CONTENTS

CHAPTER ONE

LET'S GET TOGETHER

No Man Is an Island

Have you heard the saying "Two heads are better than one?" If you've ever done a research project or worked with a group to design a video game, you know it's true. Having input and help from different people can make a project stronger and more interesting. Working together can make tasks easier. If everyone pitches in to pack the camping gear for a vacation, the job is faster and smoother. This is called collaboration. It is all about working well with others to achieve a goal.

What Is Collaboration?

When you collaborate with others, you:

-  demonstrate ability to work **effectively** and respectfully with **diverse** teams

- exercise flexibility and willingness to be helpful in making necessary compromises to accomplish a common goal

- assume shared responsibility for collaborative work, and value the individual contributions made by each team member

> **"Coming together is a beginning; keeping together is progress; working together is success."**
>
> **Henry Ford**

Global Teamwork

Technology and the Internet have changed the way we work and play in the world. Fifty years ago, most work was done by individuals working alone. Now, most important projects are carried out by teams of people. Today's instant-communications systems make it possible for those teams to be made up of people from around the globe.

21st Century Skills

Our digitally interconnected world is always changing and evolving. To keep up and be successful, we have to be lifelong learners, which means that we must be constantly learning how to think in new and innovative ways. The Partnership for 21st Century Learning is an organization that has identified four essential skills that students need to build to achieve their goals at school, at work, and in their personal lives. They are the 4Cs—communication, collaboration, creativity, and critical thinking. Each skill is important on its own, but combining the four together in our everyday lives is the key to success in a 21st-century world!

Skill Set

People may assume that they know how to work with others, but collaboration involves specific skills. It means being patient—asking for and **evaluating** each other's ideas, listening carefully, and sharing your own thoughts. Like all skills, you need to learn and practice these to work and collaborate well. Look at the list of collaboration skills. How many do you think you have?

SPOTLIGHT

Wikipedia is one of the most widely viewed websites in the world. It is a collaborative online encyclopedia, with more than 38 million articles in 290 languages. It is unique because it is written by anonymous volunteers. Wikipedia is called a "live collaboration," which means it is being changed and improved all the time by people all over the world. People of all ages, cultures, and backgrounds can create or contribute to any article, as long as they can back up their information with credible sources. The more people that work on any one article, the more complete and balanced it becomes. However, because anyone can add or change information, errors and even vandalism can creep in. Editors keep an eye on the pages, and can fix problems and inaccurate contributions.

Collaboration Skills

- giving and receiving feedback

- sharing credit with others for good ideas

- acknowledging others' skills, experience, creativity, and contributions

- recognizing the feelings and opinions of others

- expanding on the ideas of others

- being able to state your own opinions tactfully, or with awareness of others' feelings

- listening patiently to others during disagreements

- defining problems in a nonthreatening way

- supporting group decisions, even if you don't completely agree

One Step at a Time

Learning how to work effectively with others can seem to be a huge task. So what is the best way to improve your collaboration skills? Focusing on one skill at a time is a good way to make sure you have truly conquered each one. If you are practicing sharing credit for good ideas, you can check the **body language** of your teammates to make sure you are successfully getting your point across. Are they smiling because their efforts have been recognized, or are they rolling their eyes?

STEP 1   STEP 2   STEP 3

Why Collaborate?

You might wonder why we should bother collaborating at all. Why not just allow individual people to use their talent to create things? Researchers have found that diverse groups can be smarter than the smartest individual. How is this possible? The reason is that people tend to build on the ideas of others, and mistakes or flaws can be corrected by other members before they weaken or ruin a project.

Collaboration is important in all areas of our lives. At home, it helps all family members feel valued and respected. If everyone is involved in creating a schedule for chores, the result will take into account everyone's strengths and needs, and there will probably be fewer problems. A collaborative effort at school or at work results in a more successful product or project.

Water-Cooler Collaboration

Some companies deliberately hire workers who are not only good at their jobs, but also have unrelated interests. A survey of their employees might reveal people with interests in kite-making, breeding racing pigeons, glass-blowing, and roller derby! These employees might meet up over lunch or in the hallways, and have random conversations that can lead to fascinating new ideas.

Brainstorming

Brainstorming was a new idea in 1952. It is a way to find answers to a specific problem or to create something new by coming up with a list of possible ideas. Alex Osborn developed the concept when he worked in advertising to produce ideas for new ads. Brainstorming is often done by a group, but unlike collaboration, it can also be done by an individual.

Brainstorming has two rules:

1 Don't judge how good or bad an idea is when it is created.

2 Come up with as many ideas as possible.

Osborn wanted lots of ideas to be generated rather than just waiting for one good idea. He believed that the greater the number of possible ideas, the more likely it was that a unique, exciting idea would be produced.

SPOTLIGHT

Alex Osborn was born in New York in 1888. After college he worked as a journalist, then joined an advertising agency. While he worked at the agency, he became interested in the best methods of creating exciting and original ideas that he could use in advertising campaigns. He went on to write several books on creativity. In 1952 he introduced the idea of "group brainstorming," which was the beginning of the idea of collaboration.

"It is easier to tone down a wild idea than to think up a new one."
Alex Osborn

Teamwork or Collaboration?

Teamwork and collaboration are often confused. They are similar in that they both refer to groups working together. The difference lies in how the groups operate.

Teamwork

In teamwork, there is a leader who **assigns** different jobs. The leader keeps that role for the whole assignment. These jobs are all done at the same time, but they do not feed off each other. A baseball team is an example of teamwork. The coach tells each player where he will play on the field. The pitcher, catcher, basemen, and outfielders, each have a different role to play in the game. They all play together, but they stick to their job.

Collaboration

In collaboration there can also be a leader, but their job is not to hand out assignments—they are tasked with keeping things under control and moving along. Different people can take the leadership role at different times for agreed-upon periods of time. The leader and the other group members all work toward the same goal at the same time. They can bounce ideas off each other, and build on what has already been said or created.

> **"Great things in business are never done by one person. They're done by a team of people."**
> *Steve Jobs*

HANDS ON

This challenge provides an opportunity to practice collaborative problem-solving skills.

Materials needed:

One room fan, one package of building materials for each team; this can include toothpicks, elastic bands, sticky notes, pipe cleaners, construction paper, etc..

Challenge:

You are a team of Arctic explorers trekking in the frozen north. A storm is coming and you need to build an emergency shelter. However, your team leader has frostbite and can't use his hands. The rest of the team has snow blindness and can't see.

You have 15 minutes until the storm hits. The leader must direct the other members to build a model of the shelter using the materials given. Then, turn the fan on to see if your shelter can withstand a blast of cold Arctic wind!

World Music

"We Are the World" was a musical collaboration recorded by the charity USA for Africa. Michael Jackson and Lionel Ritchie collaborated to write the song. The recording of the song was an even bigger collaboration. More than 45 of the top musicians in the United States participated in the recording.

CHAPTER TWO

THE GOOD, AND THE BAD, UGLY

Working Well Together

What makes a good collaborative group? The most successful groups bring together people that have a variety of skills, experiences, backgrounds, and even education. The best creativity happens when diverse thinking comes together. The more varied the thoughts and ideas, the more creative the outcome. But groups have to be put together carefully—too many of one type of person can cause the productivity of the group to come to a screeching halt!

Too big or too small

A group that is too big makes it difficult to come to any agreement. A group that is too small means there may not be enough ideas to build on.

Too many "experts"

When too many members feel they have the most knowledge, they may be less willing to come to a compromise.

Too diverse

While members need to have different interests and backgrounds, they should also have some things in common so they feel comfortable sharing ideas with one another.

Too virtual

Members who don't meet in person, or have not met before, may not have enough of a connection with each other.

What Type Are You?

Building a **productive** collaborative group means balancing the personalities, learning styles, and work methods of multiple types of people. The best groups will have women and men of different ages, knowledge, and cultures. Group members also need a chance to form relationships with each other before starting collaborations. This will help them feel confident enough to share their ideas because the group members can feel comfortable with one another. When the group works well, collaborating can be fun—and people work harder and more creatively when they are enjoying themselves.

Expert
Comes well prepared by reading all background info.

Cheerleader
Keeps everyone motivated and on task.

Inventor
Comes up with wild and creative ideas.

Skeptic
Questions everything to get people thinking in new ways.

Social Butterfly
Makes friends with everyone and keeps the session positive.

Newbie
Newcomer who may bring fresh ideas to the subject.

Veteran
Has lots of working experience with the subject.

A Matter of Trust

One of the most important elements for good collaboration is trust. Trust is being able to rely on others, and believing that they will look out for you. This is **vital** for collaborative groups. If everyone can be trusted to do their part, groups can produce amazing things!

Trust has to exist in every part of a collaboration. Members of the group have to trust others to pull their weight and contribute equally. They have to trust that others are listening to their ideas and will offer helpful suggestions. They also have to trust that others will be respectful when giving those suggestions. Without trust, group members may not feel safe or comfortable to brainstorm ideas or voice their opinions. Trust within a group means that unique ideas and creative risks can happen in a safe space. So, trust allows for the best solutions and ideas to come forward.

"Without trust we don't truly collaborate; we merely coordinate or, at best, cooperate."

American businessman Stephen Covey

Building Trust

The best time to build trust in a collaborative group is right at the beginning. But how do you build trust?

1 Set out the rules for the collaboration. When everyone knows what is expected of them, things run more smoothly.

2 Have everyone speak to the whole group. A collaboration cannot work if people start creating groups within the group, or have private conversations.

3 Have a plan in place to deal with conflict. People are human, and arguments are likely to happen. Knowing how the group will handle it will keep conflicts from taking over the process.

4 Make sure everyone is giving feedback respectfully. Nothing will shut down creativity faster than if people feel attacked for their ideas.

HANDS ON

This activity gives you the opportunity to practice sharing ideas to reach a common goal.

Materials needed:
Pen and paper for each group

Challenge:
The plane carrying your group has crashed in a remote forest. Darkness is falling and you need to survive until rescue arrives. Get together in groups of four to six people.

Your team must choose from the room you are in only 12 items that you think will help you survive. The team must rank the items in order of importance. After 15 minutes, groups should present their items and reasoning. Each group should then decide which team they think would have the best chance for survival!

When Collaboration Goes Wrong

Collaboration is not always easy. Any time you get a group of people together to work on a project, there is the chance that problems will occur.

Whether the collaborating is done in person or online, sometimes the participants don't show up or are late. Some show up but are not prepared because they have not finished prior reading or research. Not only do these things take up the time everyone has to work on the project, but they also cause bad feelings and frustration. Once the **morale** of the group is down, it is much harder to hold on to motivation.

Make It Your Own

Think about your own behavior when you work in a group. Do you listen to others, or do you talk over them? Are you a rule-follower or a rule-breaker?

Sometimes people in a group are only interested in getting across their own ideas, and don't show respect for other people's input.

Big Egos!

Other challenges can arise once things get started, too. Some people may think that their opinions and ideas are more important than others'. They might interrupt others while they're talking. Or worse, they might dismiss others' ideas as crazy, silly, or worthless. Participants will be less likely to offer up any more ideas—and that defeats the whole purpose of collaborating!

The Right Mix

Collaboration can also go wrong because the group isn't functioning well. A group of people who are too similar or too different might not make the connections that allow them to feel comfortable. They might split off into little subgroups. This can make others feel left out and picked on. These kinds of behaviors will almost certainly result in a failure to produce the best ideas—or any ideas at all. The best way to prevent or reverse problems is to have rules for the group to follow, and a group leader to keep things on track.

SPOTLIGHT

The need to have collaboration rules in place was a lesson two scientists learned the hard way. Paul Weldon and Andrew Evans teamed up to study and hopefully reproduce an acid found on the skin of an endangered ox, which might be a natural mosquito repellent. Weldon **isolated** the acid, but he needed a chemist to try to recreate it in a lab. Teaming up with Evans seemed to be the perfect collaboration. Weldon sent Evans samples of the acid to work on. Their mistake was not putting their roles or goals for the experiment in writing. Without good communication, the experiment ground to a halt and the two scientists argued over who owned the samples. In the end, they agreed to disagree, returned the samples, and went their separate ways.

Play by the Rules

So what rules should you have in place before entering into a collaboration? Group agreements should cover everything from the beginning to the end of the project.

1. Goals

If a group doesn't know what it's working toward, it's easy for the process to fall off the track. Writing the goal down will make it clear for everyone. Goals might be "Find a way to stop bullying at school," "Design a better backpack," or "Research how to start a home business."

2. Participation

Each member needs to know what is expected of them in terms of their contribution to the collaboration. This should start off with where and how often the group will meet: "The group will meet every Tuesday at 4 p.m. for one hour." It should also set out expectations for attendance: "Notify the group leader at least an hour before the meeting if you are going to be absent." It should also cover a general idea of how long the project should take: "This is a three-month project."

3. Record-keeping

Let members know how they are supposed to record notes from the meeting, and their own ideas. This will prevent wasted time repeating what has already been said or done: "**Minutes** of the meeting will be posted on our website on Wednesdays."

4. Resources

Making sure that everyone has the same knowledge of the topic before the meeting is an important way to keep the collaboration moving forward. If **resources** online need passwords, those should be provided. If information is found in books or research papers, circulate a list so everyone knows how to access them.

5. Communication

Spell out how and when members should communicate with each other. This can include rules about contacting members outside of meetings, such as a list of email addresses and phone numbers. Or it can be a rule that there shouldn't be any contact outside of meetings. These rules should also include how to communicate during meetings. Rules can include tone of voice ("No shouting"), taking turns ("Wait until a person is finished speaking before you add your thoughts"), and even eye contact ("Make eye contact with the group when speaking").

Make It Your Own

Think of a time when you participated in a group project. In what ways did it work well? In what ways did it not work well? If you could go back in time, what rule would you create to prevent the problems you encountered?

Even More Rules!

Rules help keep the collaboration a friendly and **cooperative** experience.

6. Body language

People can comment and react to others with their body language. This can be a very obvious way of communicating without words. Sometimes people need to be reminded that negative body language, such as eye-rolling or loud sighing, can hurt others' feelings.

7. Sharing information

During the meeting, information can be shared on a computer or whiteboard, or simply in a binder containing pages of information from each member. Outside the meeting, information can be shared on a website or through document-sharing applications such as Dropbox.

8. Respect

When there are disagreements in a group setting, it is important to respect others and their opinions. Feedback needs to be constructive. That means it should be based on facts, not emotions, and help the member to improve. It should also be given in a respectful, friendly way. Helpful group rules might be to "Remember to give positive comments as well as negative" or "Never make your comments personal."

9. Diversity

Members need to keep the different cultures and backgrounds of others in mind. Certain comments and jokes can offend others. Racist and sexist remarks have no place in a collaborative environment—or any environment at all.

10. Flexibility

Working in a group requires members to adapt to changes. These changes can be as simple as the time of the meeting, or as big as the goal itself. It can also be a change in how to approach the problem the collaboration is trying to solve. A good rule for flexibility might be: "Keep an open mind."

Read the Signs...

Look at these examples of body language. What do you think they mean? Which ones would have a positive effect in a collaborative discussion? Which ones would have a negative? Why?

Make It Your Own

Body language is the expressions or **gestures** people use. It is a way of communicating without using words, and it can have a positive or negative effect. Think about your own body language. Make a chart with two columns. On the left, list emotions that you might feel while working in a group (for example, anger, surprise, amusement, boredom). On the right, list ways you can show that emotion without saying anything. This activity will help you become aware of your own body language.

Emotion	Body Language
Anger	Folding my arms Scowling

21

CHAPTER THREE

WHAT IS IT GOOD FOR?

Why Collaborate?

When collaboration is successful, great progress can be made. But there is more than one way to use this powerful tool. Collaboration can boost the speed and depth of learning, can help solve complex problems, and is a goldmine for creativity.

Learning Together

Whether you have a broad topic that needs to be looked at or a narrow topic that you need to investigate in depth, collaborative learning could be the way to go. How does it work?

1. Every member of the group learns about one aspect of the topic.
2. Participants can assist with each other's work.
3. Members present their findings.
4. Others can ask questions about the information.
5. Members can evaluate each other's ideas.

Researchers find that when people learn together, they absorb more information and gain a deeper understanding of the topic.

Instead of one person designing or creating something, a collaborative group can achieve a much better result. Alone, an individual thinks of an idea, then has to step back to evaluate it. In a group, this process can be done together, with one or more people coming up with a design, then others assessing whether it works for the project. This can result in better thought-out projects.

Creativity also increases when people feed off each other's ideas. This is especially true in music, art, and writing. Musical collaborators can listen to each other, then build on the notes and lyrics of their partner.

SPOTLIGHT

The Inklings was a group of writers that met every Thursday night on the grounds of Oxford University in England. By day, they worked as professors, historians, doctors, and poets. At night, they read their work, then the others offered **critiques** and suggestions. Members admitted that sometimes their comments were "brutally **frank**." Their collaboration worked beautifully—out of this group of writers came *The Hobbit* by J.R.R. Tolkien and *The Lion, the Witch and the Wardrobe* by C.S. Lewis.

NOW A MAJOR MOTION PICTURE

THE HOBBIT
J.R.R. TOLKIEN

In this activity, you will practice collaborative problem-solving techniques, with the goal of achieving the smallest tarp or blanket possible as a group.

Materials needed:

Open floor space; A large tarp or blanket that has enough room for a group of 4–6 people to stand comfortably

Challenge:

You are a group of shipwreck survivors who have made it to the shore of a deserted island. The tide is rising and the size of the island is shrinking. Imagine the tarp or blanket is the island. Everyone in the group must put both their feet on the tarp at the same time. Then, step off it and fold it in half. Arrange yourselves again so that everyone's two feet are on the smaller tarp at the same time. Repeat this process until the tarp is as small as possible, with everyone's two feet on it. As the tarp shrinks, you will have to come up with strategies together so that everyone fits!

HANDS ON

Decisions: Large and Small

All of us participate in problem-solving every day, whether it is at home, work, or in sports and social activities. Some problem-solving decisions are small and we can make them on our own, such as whether to take an umbrella when we go out in the morning. Other decisions are bigger and have a lasting impact on our lives, such as deciding where to attend college or university, or how to deal with bullying behavior. These are the types of problems that could benefit from the ideas and support of others.

Collaborative Problem-Solving

Have you ever tried to solve a problem yourself and found that it helped to hear the ideas of others? Sometimes other people can think of solutions that you might miss, or your ideas can build on one another. Maybe someone has had success doing something in a way you had not considered. Others can offer advice on ideas that they found didn't work.

The Collaborative Problem-Solving Route

Define the problem: Make sure everyone knows what needs to be solved and why.

Share perspectives: Listen to other's view of, or experience with, the problem. Consider what has helped or not helped in the past.

Suggest options: Here is where members can rapid-fire ideas, no matter how wild or original.

Reduce options: The group can respectfully **exclude** ideas that will not work.

Evaluate: The final list of options can be debated and ranked.

Agree: A final solution is agreed on.

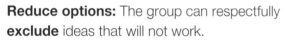

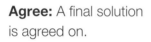

CHAPTER FOUR

COLLABORATIVE CREATIONS

Creating Works of Art and Music

Look around and you will probably see something that is the result of a creative collaboration. It could be a favorite song or a **skit**. There is no doubt that our world would be less enjoyable, less colorful, and less inspiring without collaboration in the arts. The creativity that is sparked between artists is great because it brings different styles together. This blending gives us something new and unique.

Take It Outside

Street art such as yarn bombing is the result of collaboration. Knitters and crocheters come together to cover or decorate buildings, statues, and other structures with knitted or crocheted yarn. Some consider this to be a form of **graffiti**, while other yarn bombers try to tell a story or show a theme.

Make It Up as You Go

Improv is a type of theater in which the actors come up with the script and actions while it is being performed. This is a great example of people feeding off each other's ideas. On improv TV shows such as *Whose Line Is It Anyway?* performers are given one-line suggestions and must create skits and characters collaboratively on the spot, without any written script.

Making Music

Music is a great place for collaboration in the arts. Singers of different nationalities and from different cultures and backgrounds can come together through song to send the message that we are more alike than we are different. David Bowie and Bing Crosby got together to sing a Christmas duet of "Little Drummer Boy" and "Peace on Earth." Even though they came from different generations and countries, the song became one of the most successful duets in Christmas music history.

Rodgers and Hammerstein were two talented musical theater composers. Richard Rodgers wrote the music and Oscar Hammerstein wrote the lyrics for the songs of famous Broadway shows and movies such as *The Sound of Music*, *Oklahoma*, and *State Fair*. Their partnership has been called the greatest musical theater writing team of the 20th century.

SPOTLIGHT

Not all collaborations are a good idea. Sometimes certain musical styles don't blend well, or the artists don't suit each other. Some people think the collaborative song "Accidental Racist" by hip hop artist LL Cool J and country singer Brad Paisley was an odd mix. It received a negative reaction from some fans and critics!

Innovative Ideas

Some of the most innovative products on the market today are the result of collaborations. Collaborations help in designing new products because each participant brings their own specialized knowledge to the table, helping to create something unique.

Building a Better Backpack

Need a backpack that doesn't hurt your spine after hours of carrying a heavy load? Why not get one designed by both a hospital and an office-supplies company?
A hospital in Spain specializing in children's health teamed up with a stationery manufacturer to create a better backpack. It has different compartments to balance the weight so there is less stress on the wearer's back, and safety straps that fasten across their chest.

SPOTLIGHT

When companies in very different fields come together, unusual and unique outcomes can occur. L'Oreal is a cosmetics company that develops hair dye, skin-care products, makeup, and perfumes. Renault is a car manufacturer. Renault contributed its knowledge of car features, and L'Oreal shared its knowledge of skin-cell biology, during their collaboration to create the "Spa Car." Special air filters and nondrying air conditioners in the Spa Car protect passengers' health and improve their driving experience.

Get Moving!

The products we use should change along with our lifestyles. More people tend to use technology while they are being active, but this can be damaging to our devices. The answer could be collaboration between sports equipment and technology manufacturers. Adidas is well-known for athletic footwear. Sennheiser is a German audio company that makes microphones, headphones, and other communications equipment. Together they have created high-quality headphones that are water- and sweat-resistant, for use during exercise and sports.

Make It Your Own

Think of a favorite sport or hobby, and a piece of clothing or equipment you need to participate in that activity (for example, soccer cleats, a riding saddle, or a rock hammer for climbing). Now try to come up with an innovative new product that improves the way you use the item. Think of a company that could improve the design. Perhaps a metal manufacturer could make better cleat studs, a wetsuit producer can create waterproof leather saddles, or a **trapeze** manufacturer could build a hammer handle with an easier grip.

Science Matters

Nothing has more impact on people around the world than advances in science and medicine. But scientific exploration and research to cure diseases takes a lot of time and a lot of money. How can we speed up the process to improve people's health worldwide? Collaboration is key in this field because **pooling** information, ideas, and tasks can move things forward.

A double helix looks like a twisted ladder.

Into the Body

Discovering how information is stored in our cells was the beginning of scientists unlocking the mysteries of how the human body works. Once they understood the information inside us and how it was passed from generation to generation, they could work on changing it, fixing it, or even **cloning** it.

British scientist Francis Crick and American scientist James Watson were the first to discover that the information in our cells forms in the shape of a double helix. They were credited with the discovery, but they recognized that the work of many scientists went into it. Like the best collaborations, it took the work of a diverse group of scientists and ideas to find the answer.

SPOTLIGHT

In 2010, a collaboration of 126 researchers working in 21 countries began looking for frogs that had not been seen in more than ten years. Not only did they find several kinds of frogs that people thought were extinct, they also discovered new species that were never seen before, such as the beaked toad of Colombia!

The Hunt for *Terror* and *Erebus*

For hundreds of years explorers were searching for a northern route to Asia from Europe, which they called the Northwest Passage. Sir John Franklin and his crew left England in 1845 on two ships—the *Terror* and the *Erebus*— intending to be the first to find the route. But the ships sank somewhere in the north of Canada and were never seen again.

Many attempts were made to find the lost ships. The size and **scope** of the search made it clear that this was not a job for just one organization. A collaboration was needed. The hunt for the *Terror* and the *Erebus* brought together Parks Canada, the Royal Canadian Geographical Society, Arctic Research Foundation, Canadian Hydrographic Service, Canadian Coast Guard, as well as the oral histories of the Inuit people who lived in the Arctic. The group effort paid off. In 2014, the combined **expertise** of all these groups led to the discovery of the *Erebus* off the coast of King William Island. The search continues for the *Terror*…

Collaboration in the Digital Age

Nothing is changing faster in our world than technology. In this digital age, the Internet has made collaboration easier and more productive. This is a positive step forward because technology brings together the ideas of people who are not likely to meet in person. Sometimes this is because of distance, but other times it's because our lives overlap more online, where people of different generations or cultures might meet because of common interests.

A Global Network of Doctors

The Mayo Clinic is a system of hospitals, clinics, and research facilities in the United States. With more than 3,800 doctors and scientists, they deal with the most difficult cases. But the clinic realizes that not everyone who needs this high level of care can get to one of the clinics—or even wants to. Many people prefer to be treated in their hometown by doctors they know and trust. So the Mayo Clinic has used technology and collaboration between doctors to deliver their expertise anywhere in the world. Through the Internet, local doctors can collaborate with Mayo Clinic doctors, or even a team of doctors around the world, to develop a personal plan for treating patients.

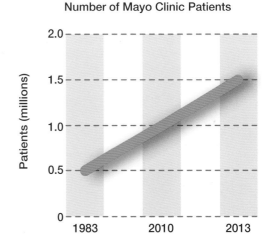

This graph shows the number of people treated by the Mayo Clinic—and the effect of its online collaboration.

Number of Mayo Clinic Patients

(Patients (millions) vs. Year)

Get in on the Game!

Collaborations online are not just for research and education—they can be for entertainment, too. You may have played video games that have an online collaborative game mode. People around the globe can join in to complete a quest, solve a mystery, or make music. *Guitar Hero 5* is one of many video games that allows people to join in and play cooperatively. Members can sing or play different instruments in the band to earn points and rewards.

Make It Your Own

With permission from an adult, find a free online group audio blog such as VoiceThread. Pick a topic you think will spark debate and conversation, such as, "What makes a hero?" Or "Are zoos a good or bad idea when it comes to endangered species?" Find images to begin your audio blog and record an opening comment that will get things going.

33

CHAPTER FIVE

COME TOGETHER

Classroom Collaboration

Almost all parts of society can benefit from collaboration. From families solving the assignment of chores in their homes to classrooms sharing their work globally to countries around the world coming together to create something incredible—collaboration is the key! School collaborations allow students to learn and solve problems together, or connect with other students around the world. This is a great way to experience cross-cultural learning. It also boosts creativity through the exchange of ideas.

Get Smart

The International CyberFair is the largest online educational event of its kind. More than 5 million students from 115 countries around the world meet online to create and share their vision of the future. Each year, students create **innovative** and unique projects in different topic areas. Students work collaboratively to do research and upload their project to the site. There is a tool so other students can evaluate their peers and offer feedback. The winners are announced in the spring, with hundreds of schools watching through the Internet.

Share What You Know!

Literacy skills can also be practiced and improved with collaborative projects. Teachers in different areas can set up new projects on sites such as GlobalSchoolNet, and invite others to join. Projects include writing workshops in which students collaborate on fiction or nonfiction writing. There are science projects dealing with current issues such as litter in the oceans and weather patterns around the world, and cultural exchange projects. The variety of topics are sure to get anyone collaborating with peers in the classroom and around the world!

Make It Your Own

Create your own collaborative work of fiction with your classmates. This can be as simple as a notebook passed from student to student, or a virtual whiteboard or shared document online. Remember to set out good collaboration rules beforehand, such as the genre of the finished work (mystery, fantasy, etc.), the length of each person's contribution, and how others can offer comments and feedback. You might write a story about a group of strangers stranded on an island, or a story that is inspired by an interesting image.

Doing Business

Businesses and organizations also benefit from collaboration. When they work together, they bring different expertise to a problem and can help each other reach new **markets** of customers. For example, a real-estate company might team up with an **aromatherapy** business to create inviting scents in houses that are for sale. This could help the real estate company sell more houses, while the aromatherapist might find new clients by displaying their products during open houses.

Getting Fit

Working out at the gym can sometimes become boring. But what if your workouts were based on the routines, music, and backgrounds created by the world's most innovative acrobatic circus? That's just what happened when Cirque de Soleil teamed up with Reebok to develop new workouts to make going to the gym more inviting. Called Jukari, it uses trapeze-like bars with loops for your arms and legs, so you can climb, swing, and fly your way to fitness!

WHEN THEY WORK TOGETHER, BUSINESSES AND ORGANIZATIONS BRING DIFFERENT EXPERTISE TO A PROBLEM.

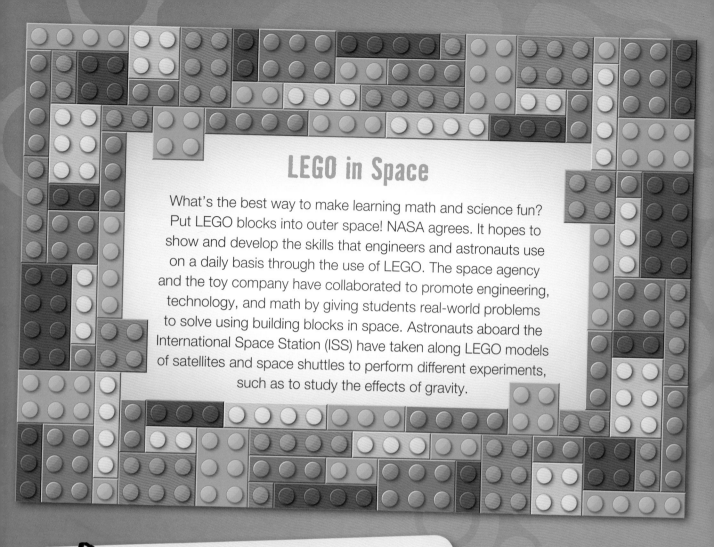

LEGO in Space

What's the best way to make learning math and science fun? Put LEGO blocks into outer space! NASA agrees. It hopes to show and develop the skills that engineers and astronauts use on a daily basis through the use of LEGO. The space agency and the toy company have collaborated to promote engineering, technology, and math by giving students real-world problems to solve using building blocks in space. Astronauts aboard the International Space Station (ISS) have taken along LEGO models of satellites and space shuttles to perform different experiments, such as to study the effects of gravity.

SPOTLIGHT

When Ben Cohen met Jerry Greenfield in their 7th grade gym class, they didn't know they would later get together and become famous for their sweet treat: Ben & Jerry's ice cream. In true collaborative form, they now have a team of "flavor gurus," who help them come up with new and unique flavor combinations. These gurus travel around the world looking for flavor inspiration by ordering and eating every dessert they find on their travels!

Country Wide

Collaborations that happen across an entire country can offer new programs or services to all citizens. This can help problem-solving in large countries, such as Canada and the United States, where people in remote areas can feel left out or are not represented in the collaboration because it is sometimes too difficult to connect with them.

Fighting Disease Together

Keeping an eye on **contagious** diseases is a difficult job in a country as large as Canada. But Canada's National Collaborating Center for Infectious Diseases (NCCID) is a perfect example of how collaborating across a country can provide a vital service—not to mention save lives! The NCCID works with doctors, nurses, public health staff, and many others, to put programs in place to identify and prevent infectious diseases across the large country.

Coordinating the flu shot program keeps the deadly disease from killing thousands of Canadians each year. Health-care providers need to collaborate to make sure the flu shot is available across every Canadian province and territory. This graph shows the number of Canadians receiving the flu shot since 2003.

Number of flu shots received in Canada

You're the Future!

The future of any nation lies with its youth. Preparing young people to meet the challenges of a changing world is the idea behind the National Collaboration for Youth (NCY) in the United States. The NCY has set up programs to develop **strategies** to prevent students from dropping out of school, help them acquire new skills, and promote leadership. They have recently partnered with Ready by 21, which is a set of strategies for communities to support their youth, ensuring that every child is ready for college, work, and life by the age of 21.

SPOTLIGHT

One goal of Parks Canada is to help people to recognize and value national parks. To help achieve this, Parks Canada collaborated with Air Canada, Google, the Canadian Wildlife Federation, Owlkids Publishers, and other companies with a goal of bringing awareness to the natural world. These organizations help to fund the "My Parks Pass," which gives all Grade 8 students across the country free access to all 200 National Parks and Historic Sites. Google's collaboration includes "streetviews" of backcountry hikes and historic battlements for a virtual visit to the parks. Even Mars Canada, the makers of Mars chocolate bars, have teamed up with Parks Canada to explore the history of chocolate in Canada at many sites.

Across the Globe

International group projects are not only the most impressive type of collaboration, they are also some of the most difficult. It is possible to connect with others around the world through the Internet, but it can be impossible to connect with people in areas where the Internet is not available. Disagreements could arise between people who have extremely different viewpoints, sometimes because of differing cultures or backgrounds. However, these examples show that with clear goals and strong rules, international collaboration can work beautifully.

STOP!

The global effort to rid the world of polio is the largest public-health project in history. Polio is a crippling and often deadly disease caused by a **virus**. There is no cure, but it can be prevented with a vaccine. The idea behind STOP (Stop Transmission of Polio) is to vaccinate every child around the world until the disease is wiped out. This involves a collaboration of health professionals, scientists, the World Health Organization (WHO), and many others. The hope of this collaborative group is to make the world polio-free by 2018.

SPOTLIGHT

Climate change and crop production are closely linked. If there is ever a worldwide crop failure, there could be mass starvation. The Global Seed Vault is a world collaboration to protect the diversity of not only food crops, but all plant life. On an uninhabited island in the Arctic Ocean, the Svalbard Global Seed Vault is an important and unique collaboration. Countries all over the world send seeds to the vault for safekeeping. To date, more than 840,000 seed samples are safely protected.

Svalbard
Global Seed Vault

International Space Station

Collaboration has now gone into space. Five different space agencies from the United States, Russia, Canada, Japan, and Europe have come together to build and run the International Space Station (ISS). The knowledge gained from experiments and experiences in space benefit all the members. The station is owned by those five countries and its use is governed by intergovernmental agreements.

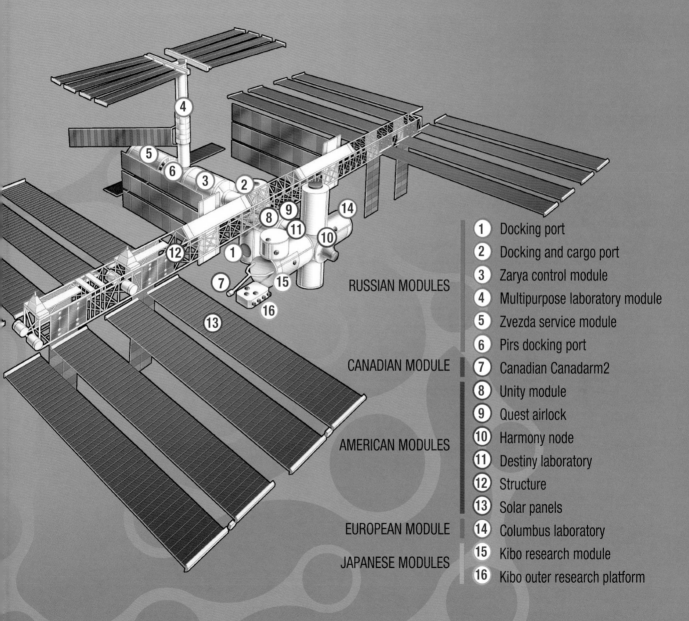

RUSSIAN MODULES
1 Docking port
2 Docking and cargo port
3 Zarya control module
4 Multipurpose laboratory module
5 Zvezda service module
6 Pirs docking port

CANADIAN MODULE
7 Canadian Canadarm2

AMERICAN MODULES
8 Unity module
9 Quest airlock
10 Harmony node
11 Destiny laboratory
12 Structure
13 Solar panels

EUROPEAN MODULE
14 Columbus laboratory

JAPANESE MODULES
15 Kibo research module
16 Kibo outer research platform

CHAPTER SIX

MAKE IT HAPPEN

Good working collaborations can produce amazing products, services, and solutions. But how can you make sure that your group will have positive results? Here are some tips for ensuring a good collaboration.

Share your thinking

Keeping ideas inside shuts the other members out. Without sharing, others can't build on, question, or improve on anything. Make it easy to share. Build trust into the group. Foster respect with rules of behavior. Try using tools that allow others to see and understand everyone's vision, whether it is low-tech paper and pens, or whiteboards and laptops.

Embrace your differences

In a diverse group, people can consider ideas and viewpoints that they might otherwise ignore. Diversity helps us explore alternatives instead of sticking to the same ideas and solutions that have been used before. Aim for a group with a mix of genders, cultural backgrounds, experience with the topic, and skills.

Be accountable

Have everyone be accountable, or held responsible, for their work. Make sure everyone knows that they are there for a reason, and their contribution is valuable. Members should feel that the positive outcome of the collaboration is due to everyone's participation. No one should hide behind others, or offer nothing to the group.

Do your homework

Come prepared to your first session. If you are the group leader, make sure you have researched the topic or problem that will be discussed, so you can talk about it with confidence. If you are a group member, it is also important to do background research. That way you will be able to offer new ideas that are based on facts, not just opinions and theories.

Limit distractions

Have the team work on one project at a time. Watch for visual or noise distractions, too. Collaborate in a space that is quiet and undisturbed by a lot of foot traffic or activity. A quiet room will allow members to focus better than in the middle of a busy library with lots of people and noise, and posters on the walls.

MAKE SURE
EVERYONE KNOWS
THAT THEIR
CONTRIBUTION IS
VALUABLE.

SPOTLIGHT

The discovery of insulin to treat **diabetes** was a collaboration at the University of Toronto between scientists, doctors, and chemists, namely Frederick Banting, John Macleod, Charles Best, and James Collip. When the discovery earned a Nobel Prize, only two of the men were recognized—Banting and Macleod. Knowing that the discovery would not have been possible without the contributions of the others, Banting immediately shared his prize with Best, and Macleod shared his with Collip.

Go with the Flow

Here are a few more tips to keep your collaboration running smoothly.

Give everyone time

People often stumble over their words when explaining their ideas for the first time. If they get a negative reaction, they may not have the confidence to continue to offer their ideas. Make sure no one feels rushed, and no one is made fun of for their thoughts and ideas. A few respectful questions can usually clear up any confusion.

Set disagreements aside

Sometimes we can't come to an agreement on something. Don't let this **derail** the whole process. Agree to set the problem aside and move forward. Confusion over, or problems with, an idea can resolve themselves with more information or with more time to reflect on it.

Disagreement time limit

If it seems impossible to set a disagreement aside, then set a limit on how much time will be given to discussing it. Sometimes things can be resolved by clearing up small misunderstandings. If nothing gets resolved before the time limit is up, move on.

Progress not perfection

It takes time to figure things out. The perfect idea or the complete solution often takes many sessions to find. Measure the success of your collaboration in terms of how much progress you are making, not how close the final solution or completed project seems.

Leave your ego at the door

Make sure members set aside their need to be "right." Collaboration is not a contest. It is not a race to see who has the most ideas, or whose idea gets the most positive feedback. To reach the goal focus on finding out what is or is not working.

Make It Your Own

Collaboration apps exist to make the process easier, but each one has its pros and cons. Make a chart to compare some of the most popular collaboration tools such as Dropbox, Google Docs, Skype, Hangouts, and Trello. Think of features such as cost, how many people can log on at one time, how information is stored, etc. That way, when it comes time for you to collaborate, you'll already have the best tools at your fingertips.

GLOSSARY

aromatherapy Using natural scents from plants to heal body, mind, and spirit

assigns Decides who will do something

body language Movements or positions of the body that show a person's thoughts or feelings

brainstorming Quickly coming up with and recording lots of ideas without judging them

cloning Making an identical copy of something

contagious Easily spread from one person to another

cooperative Involving working together to achieve a common goal

critiques Opinions or feedback on an idea, outlining what works and what doesn't

derail To block something so that it cannot achieve its goal

diabetes A disease in which the body does not produce enough of a hormone called insulin

diverse Having a lot of variety; when things are not all the same

effectively In a productive way

evaluating Assessing the value of something to see whether it is working

exclude Leave out

expertise Specialized skills or knowledge about a particular subject

frank Open, honest, and direct

gestures The movements people make, usually with their hands, to emphasize what they mean or how they feel

graffiti Writing or drawings, often on public buildings or in public places

innovative Using new methods of creating things or new and original ideas

isolated Separated out

literacy The ability to read and write

markets Any place where transactions can be made, or where there is supply and demand for products

minutes A record of what was said and agreed on at a meeting

morale The confidence and enthusiasm of a group

perspectives Viewpoints

pooling Sharing for the benefit of everyone involved

productive Able to produce, create, or make lots of ideas or products

resources A supply of information or materials

scope The extent of the area

skit A short comedy sketch

strategies Plans of action outlining how someone intends to achieve something

trapeze A bar that hangs by two ropes that is used as a swing in a circus

virus A microorganism that causes disease

vital Absolutely necessary

LEARNING MORE

Books

The Amazing International Space Station by the Editors of *YES Mag*. Kids Can Press, 2003.

Franklin's Lost Ship: The Historic Discovery of HMS *Erebus* by John Geiger and Alanna Mitchell. HarperCollins, 2015.

Wikipedia: The Company and Its Founders by Jennifer Joline Anderson. Essential Library, 2011.

Websites

Debategraph
http://debategraph.org/Stream.aspx?nid=61932&vt=bubble&dc=focus
Create a map of your collaboration with this free award-winning web platform.

GlobalSchoolNet
www.globalschoolnet.org/gsnpr/search.cfm
Pick a new collaborative project from around the world, and join an international team to achieve a goal.

International CyberFair
www.globalschoolnet.org/gsncf/
Join in the fun with the International CyberFair, the world's largest online educational event.

My Parks Pass
www.myparkspass.ca/
Find out more about this Canadian collaboration that allows schoolchildren to explore Canada's National Parks.

VoiceThread
https://voicethread.com
Start your own audio blog on this website that offers collaborative spaces for media such as audio, video, and text.

INDEX

About the Author

Natalie Hyde has written more than 50 children's nonfiction books on topics as diverse as genetics, population patterns, bioluminescence, and ninjas. She lives with her family in southern Ontario.